In The Echo Of Love

a journey where love finds our way....

Divya Dhir

BookLeaf Publishing

India | USA | UK

Dedication

Dedicated to love~
in all its messy and magnificent forms!
To the ones who love deeply, even in silence...
These poems are your voice!

Preface

Sometimes its not about the happy endings....
Its all about the story when happiness and love comes your way to find you when you have no plans to fall in love...
love finds you in the most unexpected ways at the most unexpected time...
Love has a way of echoing long after the moment has passed, lingering in glances, in silences, in the way someone says your name.
"In The Echo of Love" is born from those echoes- the feelings that refused to fade.
True love doesn't always begin with grand gestures- it often begins in small moments, quiet understandings, and the courage to be seen.

Welcome to the journey,
Welcome to the Echo.

Acknowledgements

This book is more than just ink on paper-it's a piece of my soul, offered to the world with love. Like all things born from my heart, it wasn't created alone.

Thank you, to those who held my words gently, even before they became poems and to the love that sometimes broke me, built me , gave me courage and be brave enough to achieve what I have achieved today and also gave me the sense of self love.

A heartfelt thanks to my family and friends, who believed in me even when I doubted myself. Your encouragement has been my guiding star.

To every reader who picks up this book - I am grateful beyond words. May you find a piece of yourself between the lines.

And finally, to the language of love-- Hindi and Urdu-- thank you for giving me the most beautiful words to speak my truth.

With all my heart,
Divya Dhir.

1. Phir Wahi Hai (Again, the same)

Log badal jaate hain,
Mausam ki tarah....
Aur hum yunhi mausam ke badalne ka,
Intezaar karte rahe.....

Translation (Again, the same):

People change like seasons...
And I was silly enough to wait for the season to change!

2. Badalte Mausam (Changing Seasons)

Zindagi badal rahi Hai, .
Phir bhi Har Din Wahi Hai...
Badal to aate jaate hai,...
Par barish Phir Wahi Hai...

Har din nazariya badalta hai,
Par nazarein Phir Wahi Hai...
Kashti raah badal bhi de,
Par saagar Phir Wahi Hai...

Hum khud ko gar badal bhi de,
Par ye Duniya Phir Wahi Hai...

<u>Translation (Changing Seasons):</u>

Life is changing day by day still I feel everything is the same...
Clouds fascinate me, they keep coming and going but rain is still the same...
Everyday I see something new and learn something new, but eyes are still the same...(they see what is evident but sometimes tends to miss out what is there between the layers)

Even if a ship changes its course,
ocean is still the same...
Even if we change ourselves,
the world is still the same....(and the world still find flaws
in us)
So, Just Be Yourself!

3. Mukhtalif Zindagi (Different Life)

Mukhtalif si zindagi hai,
Tazurbe bhi kam nahi....
Gehraiyon mein utar kar,
khud ko paana bhi hai,
Or khud ko kho dene ka bhi gham Nahi....

Translation (Different Life):

I feel my life is different having different experiences...
I want to go in the depth of life to find myself.
I am not afraid of losing myself...

POV : Try to know more about your soul not just your physical being!

4. Honsle Buland (Determined and Strong)

Honsle buland hon ton,
Manzilein mil hi jaati hain...
Pukhta Pedhon ki jadhon ko kya,
Hawayein daraati hai?

Translation (Determined and Strong) :

If we are strong and determined enough to find our way, we will definitely reach our destination....
Even the strong and gusty winds can't uproot a tree, if the roots of the tree are firm enough....

POV : People who are strong and their roots are grounded...the strong winds (i.e. their rivals) can't break them. If your soul is grounded, Mother Earth will hold you firmly. No one can break you.

5. Ibtida-e- Ishq (Beginning of Deep Love)

Ibtida-e-Ishq hai,
Zara dheere dheere chal....
Phoolon ke saath saath,
Kaante bhi biche nazar ayenge...

Translation (Beginning of Deep Love):

It's just the starting of love...
Go slow...
When you see closely,
you'll see thorns along the way and not just flowers

POV: Love is an illusion ...when it's blooming...one should be slow and careful...as there are so many unknows and problems on the way along with it's charm)

6. Kahaani (Story)

Yun tumhara nazarein milakar chura lena,
hamein berukhi nahin lagti...
Nazron mein chupi kahaani aksar,
dilchasp hoti hai....

Dhaage me piroya moti,
behad khoobsurat hota hai magar,
seep mein chupe moti ki baat hi kuch or hoti hai....

<u>**Translation (Story):**</u>

When you look into my eyes and then look away...
I don't feel that it's your arrogance....
People who hide love in their eyes always have an
interesting story....
Like a pearl in a necklace looks beautiful but the beauty
of pearl inside the sea shell is beyond words!

POV: People who expresses love through eyes, love
deeply. A deep person is a rare person.

7. Waqt Aur Mausam (Time And Seasons)

Mausam waqt se puchta hai,
Tu kyu baar baar badalta hai....
Waqt kehta hai meri to fitrat hi badalna hai,
Par tu kyu apni adat badalta hai....

Insaan bhi badalta hai mausam ki tarah,
Kabhi nazar badalta hai, Kabhi imaan badalta hai....

Kaise karein bharosa kisi par,
Kabhi koi baat badalta hai, aur kabhi jazbaat badalta
hai....

<u>Translation (Time And Seasons):</u>

The weather is personified and inquisitively asks Time
(also personified), "Why do you keep changing?"
Time replies, "Change is my very nature. But tell me,
Weather — why do *you* change so often?"
People are like the weather too — always changing.
Sometimes they change the way they see things.
Sometimes, they change who they are.
So how can you trust anyone, when what they say and
what they feel Keeps changing all the time?

8. Puraane Khat (Old letters)

Aj mile kuch khat puraane,
Dil ke kareeb the kuch afsaane...

Lafzon ki gehrai mein,
Yaadein beh rahi thi...
Maine thodha nazdeek jakar dekha ,
To kuch mjhse keh rahi thi...

kehti hain mujse us kal mein chal,
wo kal jo apna sa lagta hai...
Magar kya karun jakar wahan,
Na log hai apne, aur na hi kuch apna sa lagta hai...

Translation (Old letters):

Today, I found some old letters that were close to my
heart...
So many memories started flowing in the depth of
words...
Those letters were trying to convey something, as if they
wanted me to go back in time...
But what should I do going back in time, when the
people who were then mine are not mine anymore and
everything seems to be different now...

9. Galat Fehmi (Misunderstanding)

Tumhe lagta hai,
Meri zindagi mein gham nahi....
Chalo tumhari galat fehmi ko,
apni muskurahat mein chupa loon....

<u>Translation (Misunderstanding):</u>

You feel that I do not have anything to worry in my life..
Though its not true, I'll let that feeling prevail by smiling
when around you.

10. Aankhein (Eyes)

Tumhari aankhon mein jeena chahti hoon mai,
Bin piye hi peena chahti hoon mai...
Tumhari aankhon mein gum ho jaun agar,
Kasoor mera nahi mai kho jaun agar....

Translation (Eyes):

I want to live in your eyes...
I long to drown...without the wine touching my lips...
It won't be my fault if I get lost in your eyes....

11. Khwabeeda (Dreamy)

Khwabeeda Mizaaj rakhti hai ye Shayara janaab...
Tum to udhte ho hawa jaise,
mujhe kya samajh paoge....

Taabir mere khwaabon ki,
itni asaan bhi nahin...
mere lafzon ki ruhaniyat mein,
tum kya utar paoge.....

<u>**Translation (Dreamy):**</u>

I (The Poetess), have a daydreaming nature....
You (My Love) are so busy in your fast life ....
But I Live a slow life living and experiencing every
moment...
How will you be able to understand me when we have
two different worlds...

Interpretation of my dreams is not that easy....
You won't be able to understand the depth of my
words.....

12. Pyar (Love)

Pyar jo ibaadat se kam nahi..
aj bas kitabon mein likha acha lagta hai..

Aj logon ko khud se hi fursat nahi,
wo kya karenge pyar kisise,
jinhe bas khud ke bare mein sunna acha lagta hai..

Translation (Love):

Love is not less than a prayer, but now a days it's only
good to read in books.
Today, people are so obsessed with themselves, how can
people love others when they are so into themselves.

13. Nigahein (Eyes)

Na jaane kya dhoondti hain ye nigahein,
Kuch ajnabee se chehre or kuch ajnabee si raahein...
Kisi safar ki talaash mein hain,
Ya shayad kisi gehre se sawaal mein hain...
Na jaane kis kahaani ka hissa hain ye Nigahein....

Kitni masoomiyat se ye duniya ko dekhti hain,
Par mayoos ho jaati hain...
jab koi nigahein inhe parakhti hain....
Phir bhi saadgi lekar chalti hain...
Na jaane itni mukhtalif kyun hain ye Nigahein...

<u>Translation (Eyes):</u>

I don't know what my eyes are looking for? I see
unfamiliar faces and unknown roads....
Either they are looking for a different journey or they are
looking for some answers....
I don't know where my eyes are entangled or a part of
which story.....
They look around the world so innocently....
But they get disappointed when people instead of
knowing them starts judging them...
I don't know why my eyes are so different...

14. Khwaab (Dream)

Tum yaad ho mujhe ek khwaab ki tarah,
Ki jab bhi mai chaand ko dekhti hun mjhe tum hi nazar
aate ho...
Nahi waqif is haqeeqat se ki,
ye khwaab hai ya tasavur mein bani koi tasveer,
haan main jab bhi aaine mein khud ko dekhti hun,
Mjhe tum hi nazar aate ho....

Translation (Dream):

I remember you like a dream...
Whenever I see the moon, I see you...
I don't know the reality that whether its a dream or you
are just a picture in my imagination....
Whenever I look in the mirror...
I see you...i.e. I see you in me...

15. Baarish (Rain)

Ye baarish kitni khubsurat hai,
iski bhi koi kahaani hogi....
Bhige bhige raaste pe vo intezaar kar rahi thi uska,
Shayad koi to deewani hogi...

Vo aya uske jaane ke bad,
shayad uski talaash mein....
Dhundta hua yahan wahan shayad,
Kahin uski koi nishaani to hogi...

Ye baarish kitni khubsurat hai,
Magar iski koi kahaani to hogi....

<u>Translation(Rain):</u>

The Rain looks so beautiful,
It must have a story....
She was waiting for him in the rain...
She might be deeply in love with him...

He came searching for her after she was gone,
He looked for her but couldn't find her....
He looked for some sign she might left for him....
The rain is so beautiful, It must have a story.....

16. Ishq Sufiana (Unconditional Love)

Duniya ki bandishein todh kar chala hoon,
Hoon musafir sab chodh kar chala hoon...
Talabgaar hoon is zindagi ka mai,
Ishq Sufiana bas ordh kar chala hoon...

<u>Translation (Unconditional Love):</u>

I have walked away, breaking the chains of the world...
I am a traveler...I have left everything behind....
I am a seeker of life....
I have nothing but love inside my heart....

17. Aadat (Habit)

Aadat thi yunhi tanha safar karne ki,
Isi aadat mein maine apna ghar banaya hai...
Ye mehfilein mere kis kaam ki,
Jab khamoshi mein hi maine sukoon paya hai....

Hoon to mai bs isi duniya ki,
Par maine iss duniya ko nahi apnaya hai...
Jis duniya ne aadmi ko aadmi nahin,
khilona banaya hai....

<u>Translation (Habit):</u>

I was in a habit of walking alone in the journey of life...
I have made my habit my home...
The crowd and celebrations are of no use to me...
I find peace in silence...
I am from this world but still always felt that I don't
belong in it...
This world has made humans, a puppet in its hands.....

18. Khamoshi (Silence)

Khamoshiyon ko gaur se suna karti hu mai,
Kai sawaalon ke jawaab usme dhunda karti hu mai...
Log samajhte hain mjhe baatein karni nahi aati,
Kya bataun kin ehsason ko roz jiya karti hu mai...

Translation (Silence):

Sometimes, I like to hear silence....
I search answers to my questions in silence...
People say that I don't talk much...
How should I express the flood of emotions I go through
everyday....

19. Bewaqt (Out Of Time)

Bewaqt nahi milta kuch zindagi mein,
Waqt bhi waqt ka intezaar karta hai....
Zindagi mein kuch pal gham ke,
Aur kuch khushi ke....
Insaan kabhi inhe kaed or kabhi riha karta hai.....

<u>Translation (Out Of Time):</u>

In life, we don't get anything out of time...
Time also waits for time...i.e...good time changes to bad
time and bad time changes to good time....
In Life, we have moments of both happiness and
despair....
People either let go of the moments of sadness or keep
them as memories .....

20. Farq (Difference)

Mujhe koi farq nazar na aya,
Azaan mein or mandir ki ghantiyon mein....
Na jaane kyu log baant dete hain khuda ko,
Duniya ke alag alag rangon mein...

Manzil ek hai to kyu gumraah ho jaate hai,
zindagi ki alag alag galiyon mein....
Sab yahan lambe safar ke hain musafir,
bas badh rahe hain alag alag kashtiyon mein....

<u>Translation (Difference):</u>

I don't find any difference between 'Azaan' i.e. the way
the Muslim's pray & 'Mandir ki ghantiyon' i.e. the way
Hindu's pray...
I don't know why people divide God into different colors
of the world...
When destination is same & one...why people get lost in
different paths...
All are travelers of long journeys in this world...
They are just heading to the same place but in different
ships...

21. Kalakaar (Artist)

Kalakaar hoon bs kala ko janta hoon,
Sirf tasveer hi nahin,
uske piche chupe jazbaaton ko jaanta hoon....

Sirf main hi is duniya mein nahi rehta,
Ek alag hi duniya mujh mein rehti hai...
Besabab baat har baar nahi hoti janaab,
Kuch bewajah baaton ke piche wajah ko janta hoon....
Kalakaar hoon bs kala ko janta hoon.....

<u>Traslation (Artist):</u>

I am an artist, I only understand art.
I not only see the picture, but I also understand the
feeling behind it.
Not just, I am living in this world, but a whole different
world lives inside me.
Every conversation is not unreasonable, some of them
have a deep meaning hidden inside it.
I am just an artist, I only understand art.